This book belongs to

....

MILK
XOXO

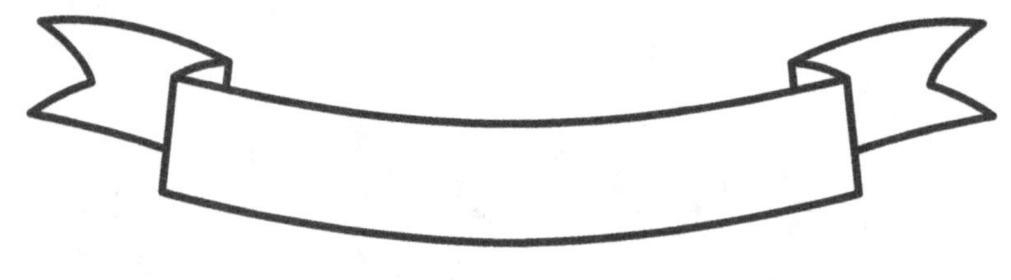

magic
Set
2

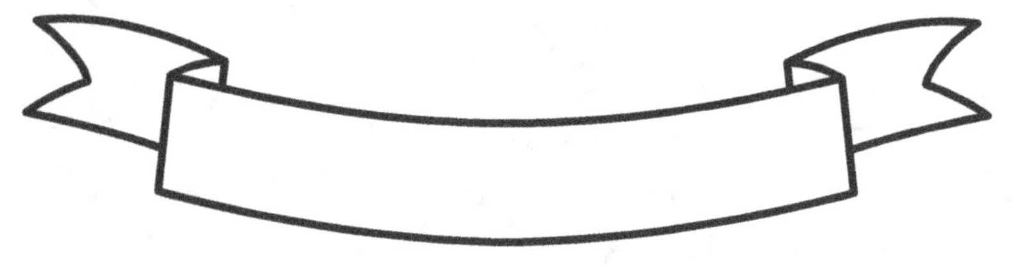

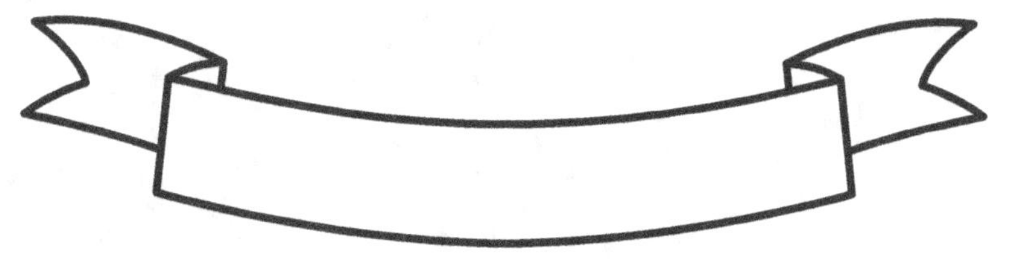

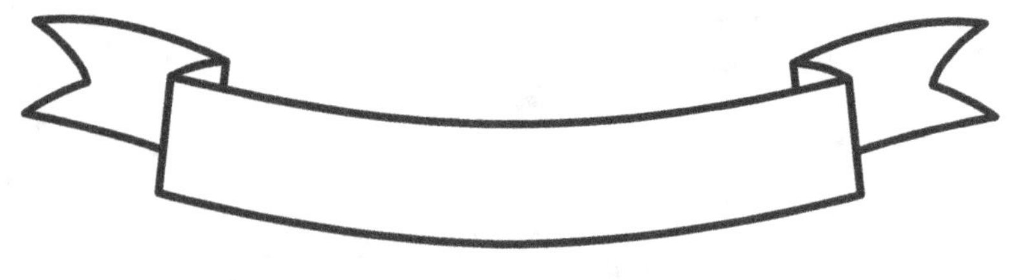

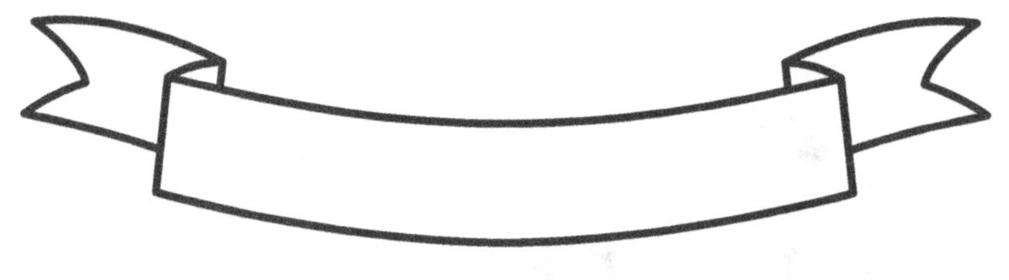

fairy tale*

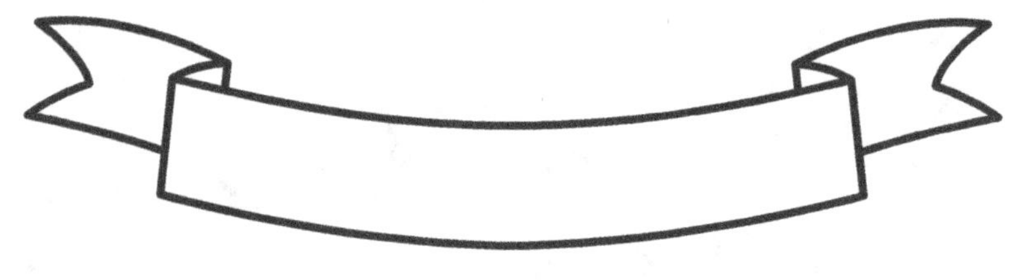

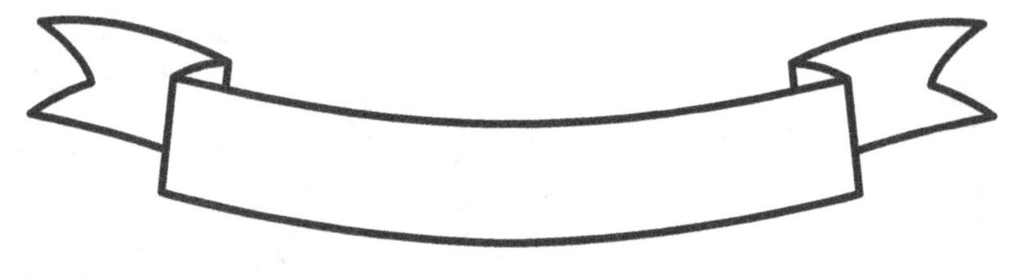

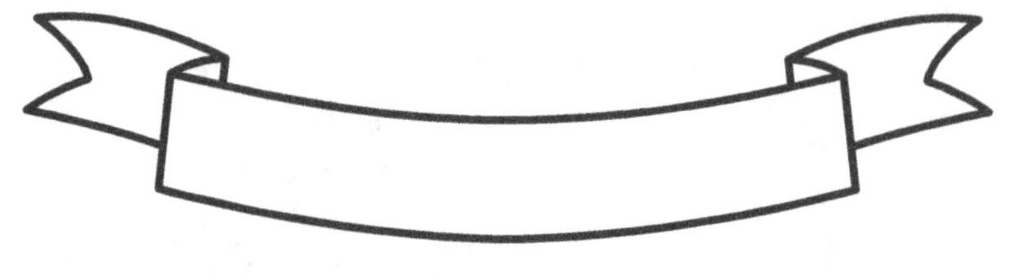 

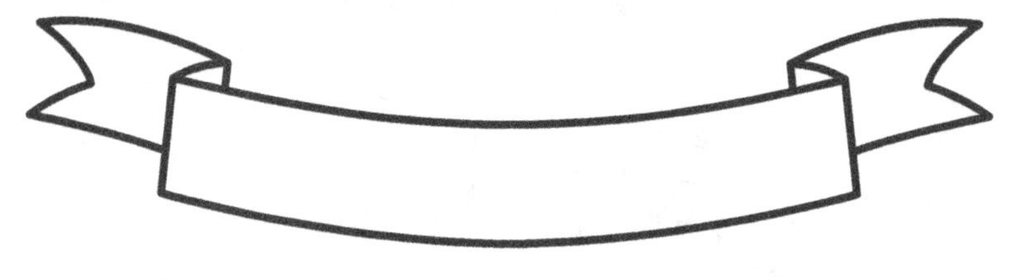

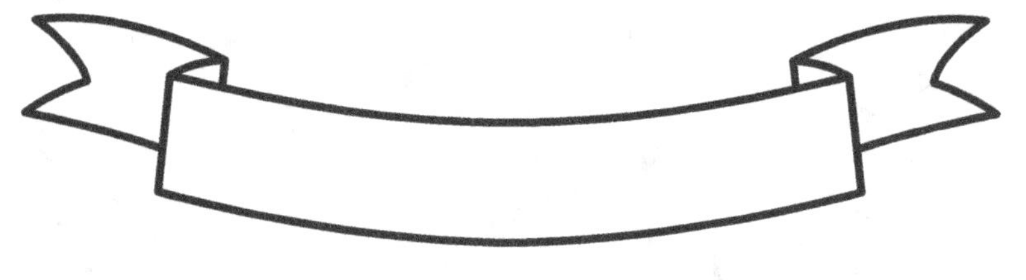

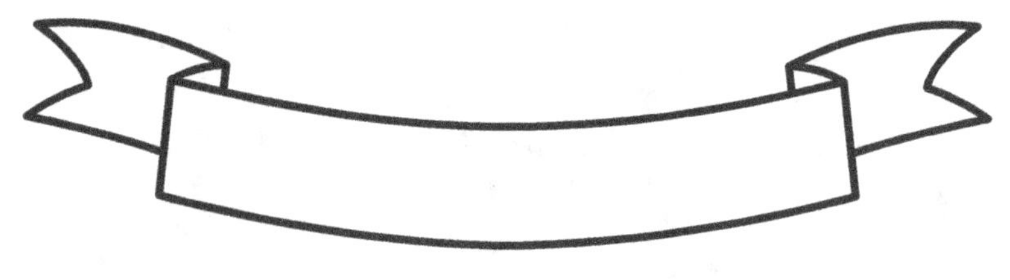

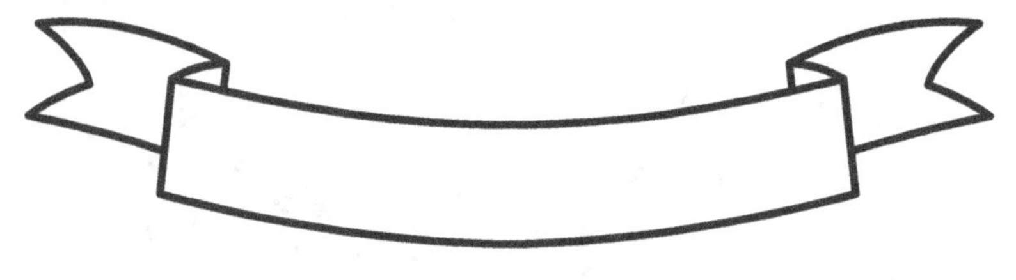

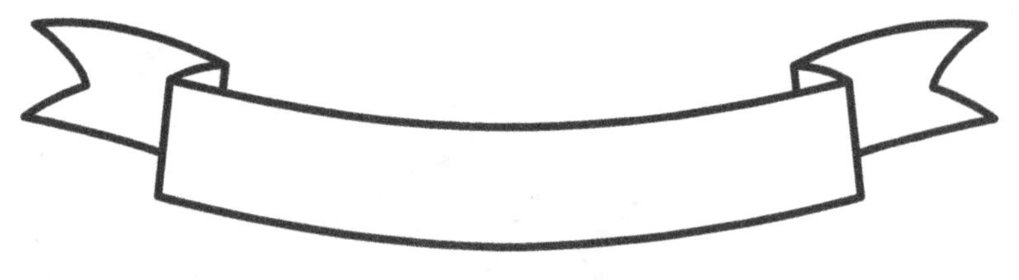

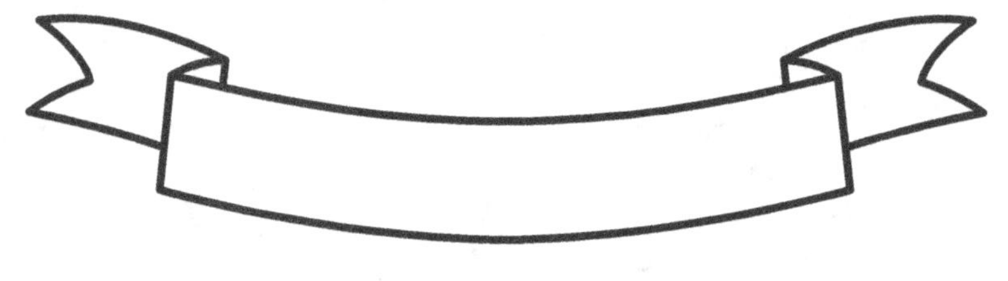

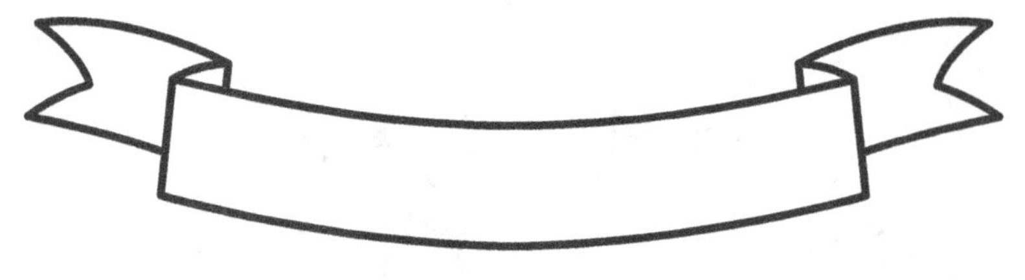

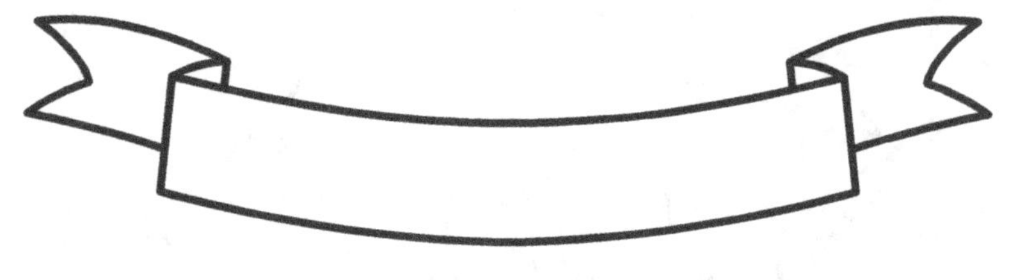

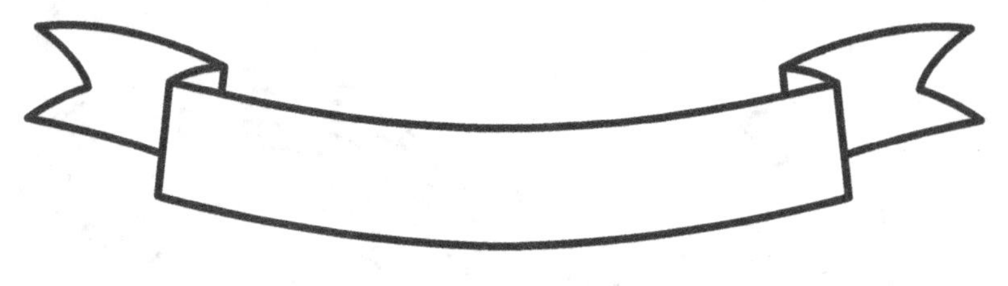

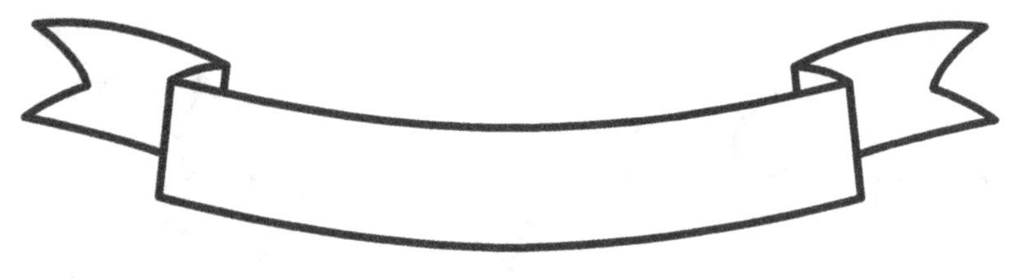

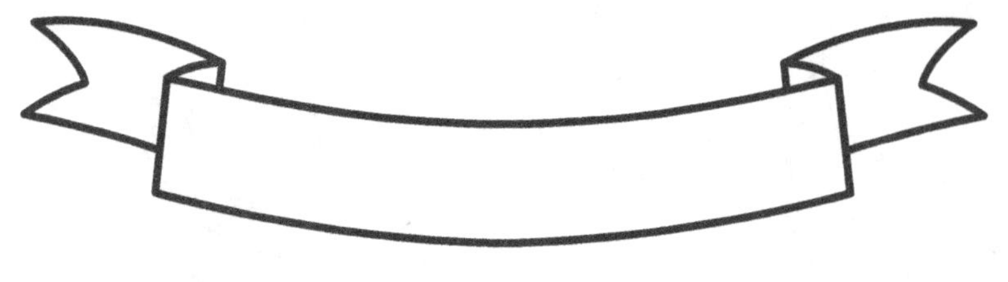

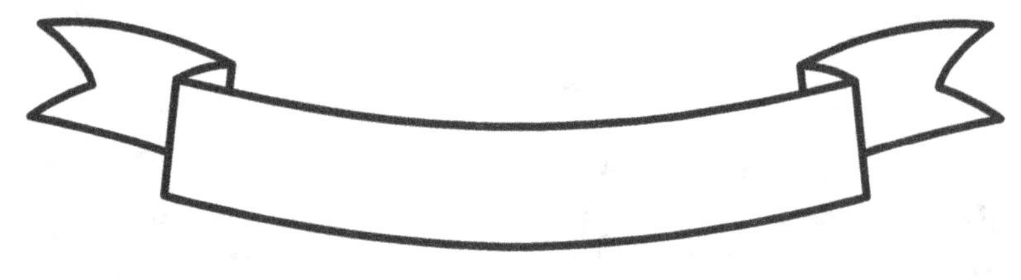

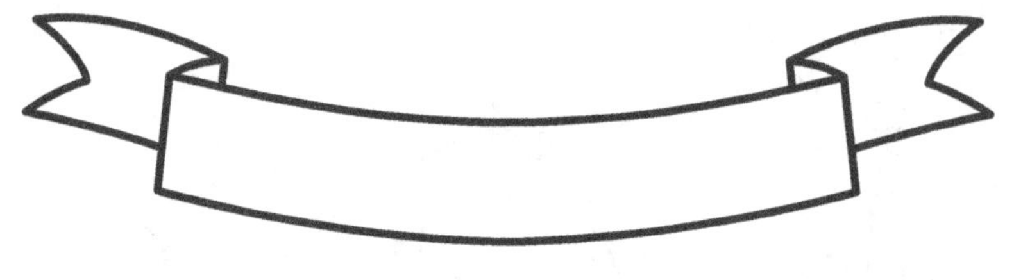

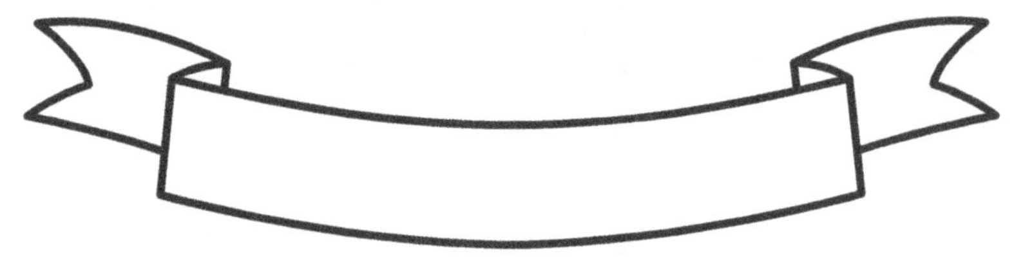

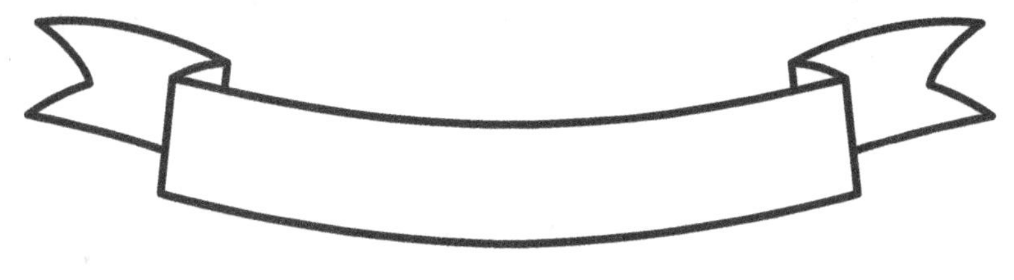

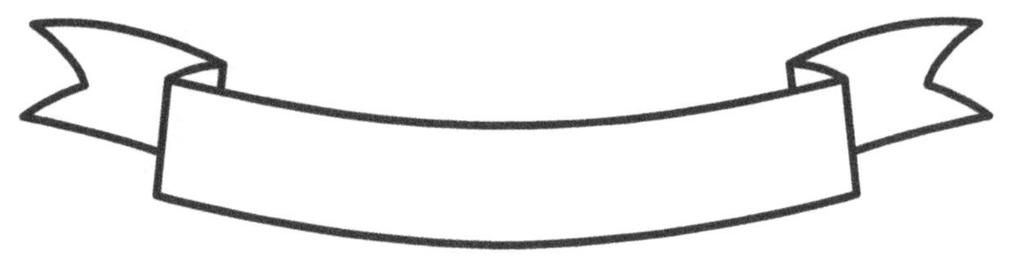

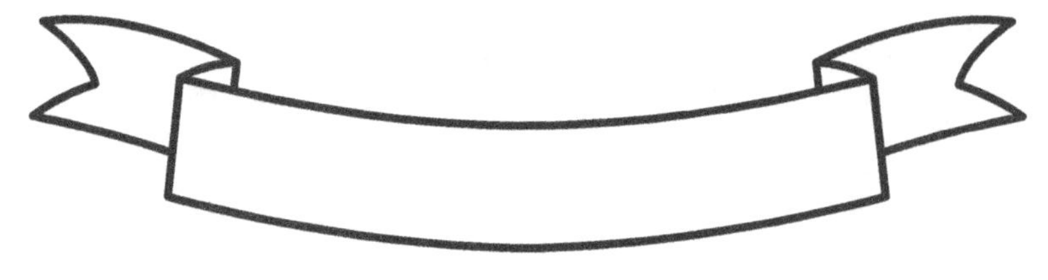

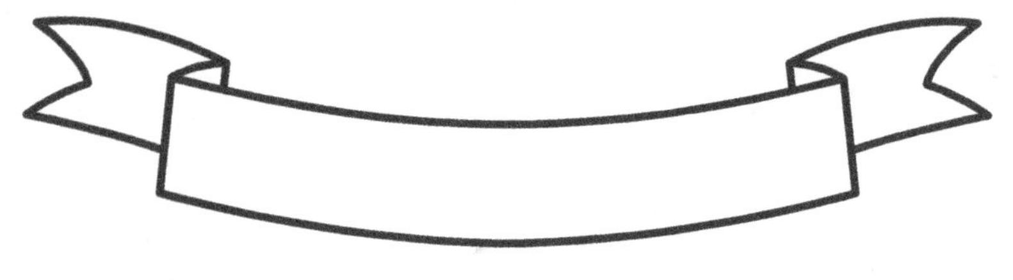

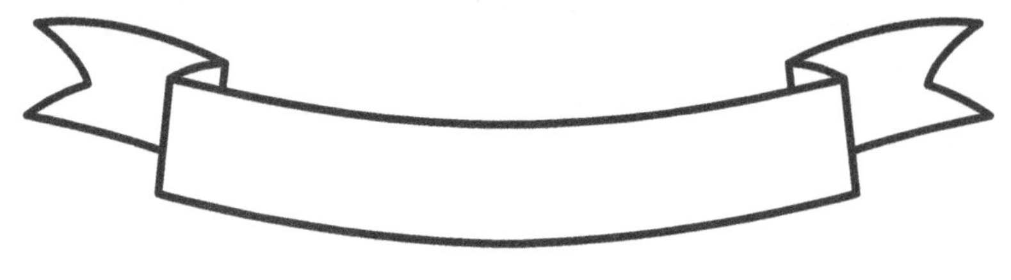

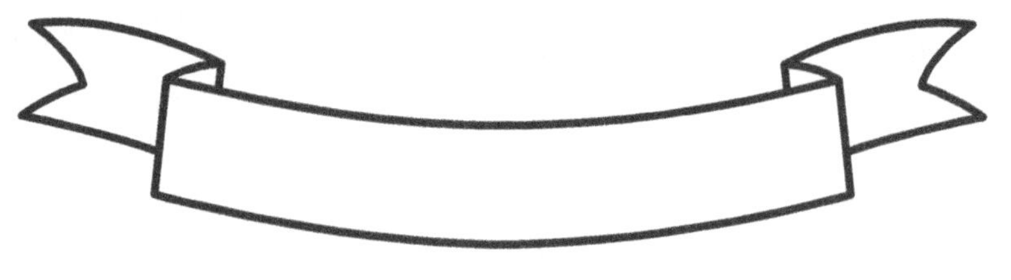

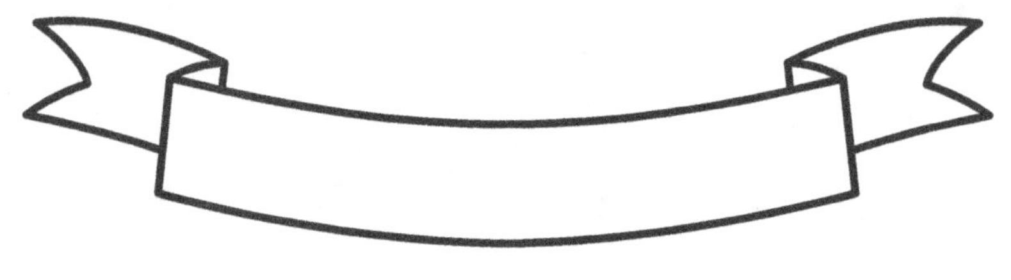

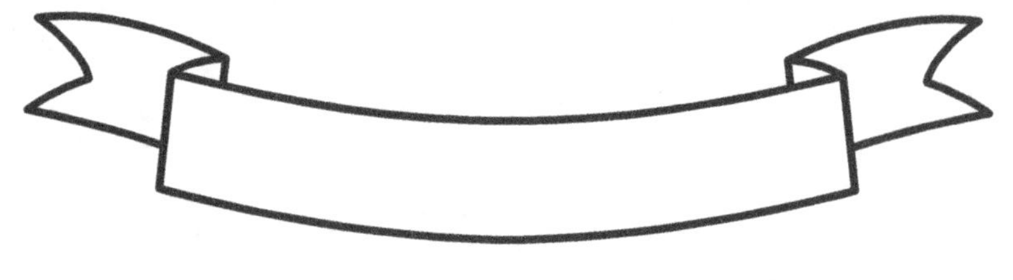

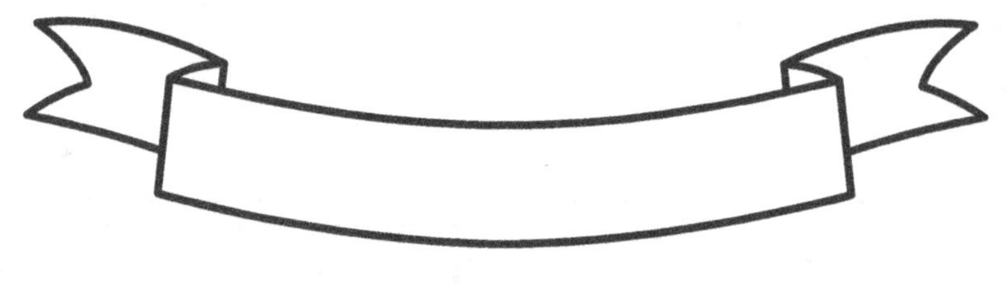

Unicorn

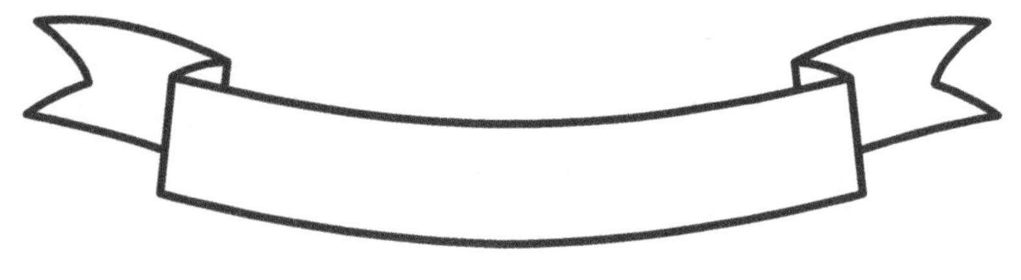

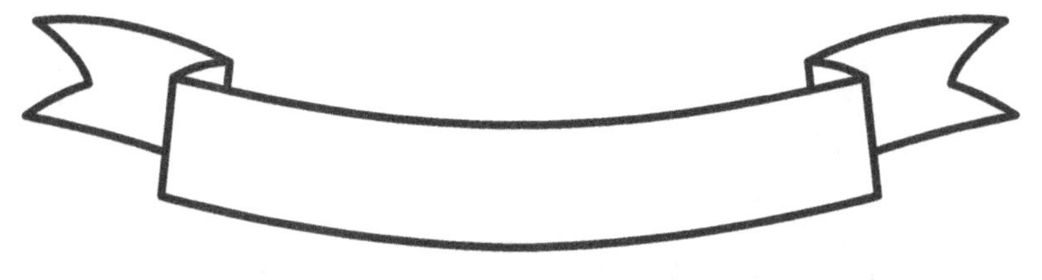

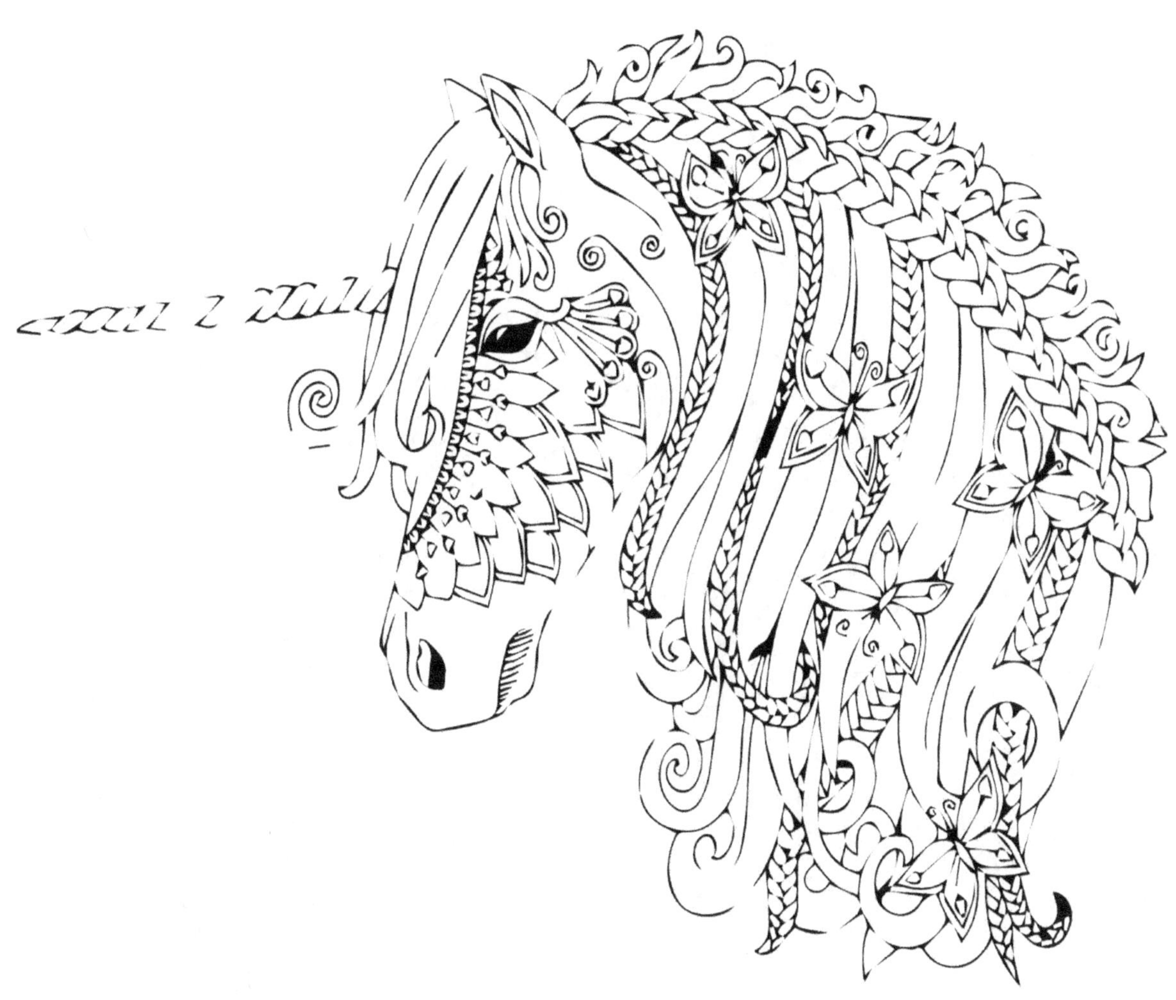

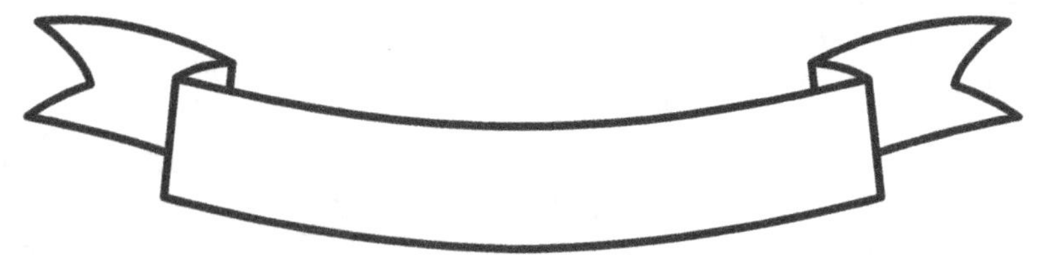

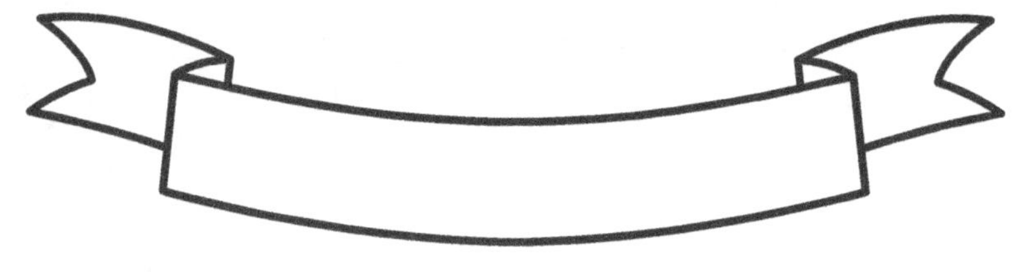

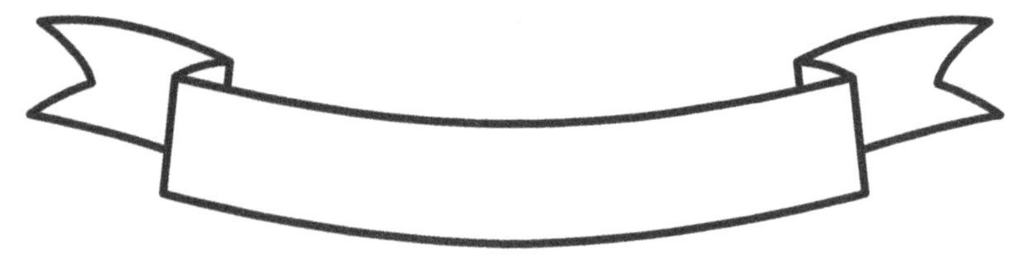

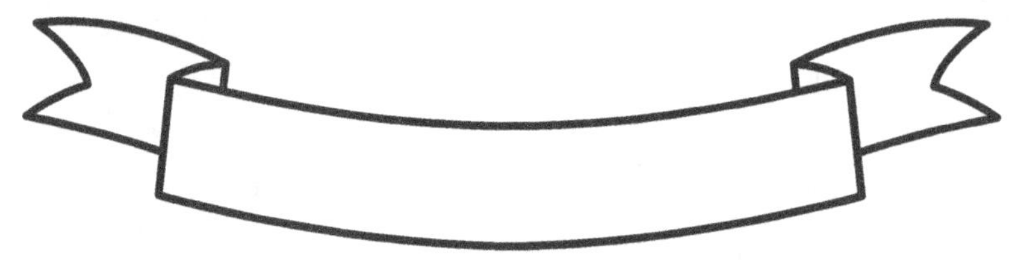

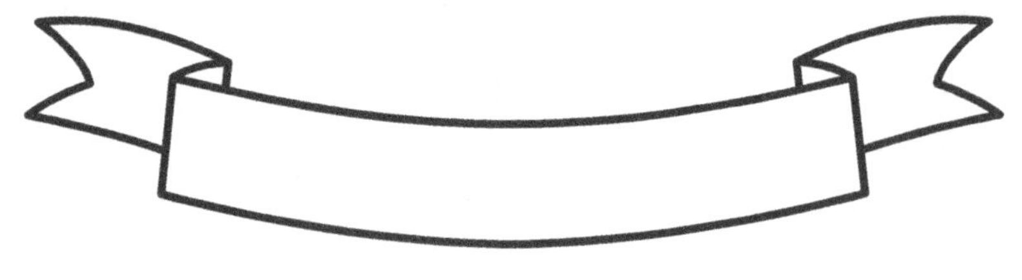